G000143588

A Director's Guide

Managing desktop IT

HOW TO SELECT PROVIDERS
OF DISTRIBUTED IT SYSTEMS
AND SERVICES

Editor, Director Publications: Tom Nash
Managing Editor: Lesley Shutte
Consultant Editor: Marc Beishon
Sub-Editor: Caroline Proud
Production Manager: Victoria Davies
Head of Business Development: Simon Seward
Design: Halo Design
Chairman: Tim Melville-Ross
Managing Director: Andrew Main Wilson

Published for the Institute of Directors and Computacenter (UK) Ltd
by Director Publications Ltd
116 Pall Mall London SW1Y 5ED

Editorial: 0171 766 8910
Sponsorship: 0171 766 8885
Production: 0171 766 8960
Facsimile: 0171 766 8990

Price £9.95

YOURS TO HAVE AND TO HOLD
BUT NOT TO COPY

Apart from any fair dealing for the purposes of research or private study, or criticism or review, as permitted under the Copyright, Designs and Patents Act, 1988, this publication may only be reproduced, stored or transmitted, in any form or by any means, with the prior permission in writing of the publishers or, in the case of reprographic reproduction, in accordance with the terms and licences issued by the CLA. Enquiries concerning the reproduction outside those terms should be sent to the publishers at the undermentioned addresses:

Director Publications Ltd
116 Pall Mall
London SW1Y 5ED

Kogan Page Ltd
120 Pentonville Road
London N1 9JN

© Director Publications 1998

British Library Cataloguing in Publication Data
A CIP record for this book is available from the British Library
ISBN 0 7494 2976 3

Printed and bound in Great Britain by St Ives plc

Contents

INTRODUCTION   **Directors and the desktop** 5
Tim Melville-Ross, Director General,
Institute of Directors

FOREWORD   **Desktop IT comes of age** 7
Mike Norris, Chief Executive, Computacenter

1   **Building your strategy** 9
Marc Beishon offers a framework for strategic decision-making

2   **Selecting your supplier** 19
Part one: tenders and contracts
Annie Gurton advises on how to choose the company that will provide your system

3   **Selecting your supplier** 27
Part two: assessment and decision making
Nick Langley argues that the key to successful selection is communication

4   **The art of IT planning** 35
Peter Lorant advises on meeting your present and future IT needs

5   **Getting the right kit** 43
Peter Bartram highlights procurement pitfalls – and how to avoid them

6   **Practice made perfect** 50
Peter Bartram looks at how two companies set about successful implementation

7   **Cutting the cost of user support** 57
Annie Gurton stresses the need to make support an integral part of IT planning

8   **Lessons in training** 65
Nick Beard explains how to ensure that staff gain the maximum from training investment

9   **The case for out-tasking** 72
Nick Langley outlines the benefits of out-tasking

GLOSSARY 80

ABOUT THE AUTHORS
Marc Beishon, Annie Gurton, Nick Langley and Peter Bartram are independent business writers specialising in the field of technology. Peter Lorant is services marketing manager at Computacenter and Nick Beard is Computacenter's head of training.

3

Directors and the desktop

Tim-Melville Ross, Director General, Institute of Directors

In today's business world, it is information technology that is driving organisations more rapidly than any other single factor. And within organisations, IT manifests itself most obviously in the form of the ubiquitous desktop personal computer. And yet most of the companies that have opted for the mass deployment of PC technology have done so as part of a gradual, incremental, inevitable process of automating their various business processes. Relatively few have considered, let alone got fully got to grips with, managing desktop computing from a strategic point of view.

Many businesses still use basic terminals connected to a central machine and do not take full advantage of the enormous benefits that the power and flexibility of current technology can bring. As a result, the same companies miss vital business opportunities and waste tens of thousands of pounds in inefficiencies. It is the responsibility of board directors in general – not only IT directors – to recognise and exploit the potential of the desktop technology now available to them.

However, directors cannot be expected to know all the answers in this complex area. The key to success in this field – as in so many others – is to tap into the right sources of information, advice and assistance. This Director's Guide will prove an invaluable starting point. It covers all the key points that need to be considered when forming and implementing a strategy for managing desktop computing effectively and cost-efficiently. And if there is one salient point within the guide, I would suggest that, in a nutshell, it is to select "best of breed" suppliers. We are living and working in a competitive world where "core competencies" have become the watchwords. Second best simply will not suffice.

We have produced this Director's Guide because our members have asked us for precisely this sort of information, in the practical, tried and tested guide format. In a recent survey of IoD members on the subject of information technology, more than one in three respondents specifically requested more Director Guides to help them solve the IT challenges they face in the rapidly moving worlds of business and technology.

We are, of course, particularly grateful to Computacenter for helping us to bring this information to a broad business readership, including all 45,000 decision-makers who make up the IoD's UK membership.

Desktop IT comes of age

Mike Norris, Chief Executive, Computacenter

In today's business world, the success or otherwise of an organisation's IT strategy is increasingly determined at the "desktop".

By "desktop" we mean, simply, computer technology that is configured for direct use by employees. Typically, this will be a personal computer, wired via a network to other computers. But although PCs are in widespread use in many businesses, the full potential of these distributed IT components is, in many cases, yet to be realised.

The reasons for this are manifold: the effective use of PCs, servers and networks can be highly complex, and brings to the fore a host of cultural, support and cost issues. "Technology churn", as today's hardware and software is continually superseded by new, more powerful products, is yet another challenge.

Increasingly, the crucial battleground for all organisations lies in the business-critical, "customer-facing" activities that demand sophisticated solutions – such as high-tech call centres and electronic commerce systems that unite the supply chain. "Back-office" systems, too, cannot be left to decline in the brave new world of integrated trading.

Computacenter has been providing desktop services since 1981. It is our task to monitor the ever rapid changes in technology, interpret the implications for our customers and offer IT products and services that meet their business needs. But for a company to maximise its investment it must adopt an IT strategy that addresses the entire IT lifecycle, ie. from Planning of IT projects through to the Requisition of hardware and software, to successful Implementation and subsequent support and Management. All of these core issues are encapsulated in the PRISM model, developed by Computacenter.

Each of the "PRISM" elements is covered in this Director's Guide, providing readers with expert advice on how to make the right choices. As a starting point, the guide highlights the value of setting appropriate standards and service level agreements that will smooth the way for the definition of desktop IT projects, and it offers advice on tendering and the supplier selection process.

Subsequent chapters address the strategic themes of planning and product selection – with case studies of successful implementations – and summarise the increasingly important role of "out-tasking" – a term allied to outsourcing, but where the company utilises the knowledge and resources of selected third-party partners, while retaining full control of its IT strategy and direction.

Computacenter is dedicated to working in partnership with its customers to deliver the best, most appropriate IT solutions. With our help, we trust this Director's Guide will be a step towards achieving greater, demonstrable value from your organisation's ongoing IT investment.

Chapter 1

Building your strategy

Choosing and implementing desktop IT systems on time and within budget is difficult, but not impossible. Marc Beishon, technology writer, looks at the framework for decision making

Over the past few years, there has been considerable concern that the costs of desktop IT are spiralling. In many companies – even some of the larger ones – the absence of a real, comprehensive IT strategy has seen the desktop system "evolve" in a random, ad hoc way. Users have been given increasingly powerful computers, packed with advanced software and networking capabilities, whether they really needed them or not.

PERSONAL COMPUTERS
Too often, a culture has developed in which the term "personal computer" has been taken literally – to mean a machine that belongs exclusively to an individual and should therefore run the applications he or she wants, regardless of their direct relevance to his or her job or the changing needs of the organisation. In addition, the fact that PCs are distributed around organisations and often installed in a piecemeal way has tended to keep capital expenditure on desktop IT "hidden" or difficult to keep track of.

Such lack of control reflects a bigger issue than the failure to impose discipline on procurement departments and work towards clear IT goals. Despite the fact that the benefits that powerful desktop systems can bring to a business are clear, there is no obvious model for a worthwhile desktop strategy.

The huge variation in desktop environments across industry and commerce makes a detailed model difficult to build, particularly in technological terms. And the list of precedents is not vast: even as we approach the millennium, there are still large-scale operations running on what can only be described as old technology – using either dumb terminals and mainframes or expensive PCs "cut down" to run simple emulations from mainframes. In this guide we aim to show that there is no reason why organisations cannot adopt desktop systems that are cost-effective, easy to control and support and can add real value to an organisation's business.

PROBLEMS AND SOLUTIONS

As a start, it is helpful to look at some of the problems that dog desktop projects and systems. These fall into two broad categories:

■ *Occupational hazards facing any modern IT manager;*

■ *Impediments that management at the top of the company can help to remove.*

The table below identifies which is which in order to highlight some of the problems that can be solved or avoided.

POTENTIAL PROBLEMS
Occupational hazards facing any IT manager
■ Skills shortages;
■ The rapid rate of technological change;
■ The fact that some products are not instantly available;
Impediments that senior management could help solve
■ Lack of resources in the IT department;
■ Lack of standards;
■ Lack of senior management buy-in;
■ Escalating support costs;
■ Increasing complexity;
■ Delays in project roll-out and time to desk.

Many of the problems in the second set stem from a wider, cultural issue: the dichotomy between business and IT managers, which is usually reflected at grassroots level in a divide between end users and the people whose job it is to give them technological support.

A recent market research survey by the software supplier Cincom Systems found that only 17 per cent of companies have an IT director on the board. Given the millennium bug and the fact that IT is increasingly business-critical–think, for example, of financial trading environments and telesales call centres – this is a worryingly low figure.

Closely linked to the failure to recognise the importance of IT is a failure to understand the issues involved. Typically, user departments are demanding not only ever higher levels of performance – accelerating the rate of technological obsolescence – but also unrealistic "time to desk" project roll-outs. The perception is that PCs are off-the-shelf items that can be installed and up and running in minutes when, in fact, a distributed network of client/server systems running many applications, a mix of operating systems and a variety of hardware platforms, can be many times more complex than a mainframe system running a standard set of applications.

Users sometimes fail to appreciate that changes to one part of the network may have knock-on effects elsewhere. And, as desktop systems increase in complexity, business departments are presented with escalating IT support costs.

TOTAL COST OF OWNERSHIP

Although the thinking behind total cost of ownership (TCO) models (see chapter 4) is fairly refined now, financial directors can sometimes be less likely to recognise the pivotal issues than their IT counterparts. Whereas senior managers in some sectors, such as financial services, demonstrate a relatively high level of awareness, others do not appreciate the benefits of analysing the true costs of distributed desktop systems.

Lack of support and understanding from other senior personnel often means IT managers are left with insufficient resources. It is not unusual to find IT departments engaging in a good deal of "firefighting" – dealing with a never ending stream of urgent user concerns, despite the presence of costly helpdesks – rather than planning the strategies that will help the business sustain competitive advantage. By out-tasking IT processes or projects, companies can free themselves from many of these headaches (see chapter 9).

IT managers also face the problem of keeping up with the rapid pace of technological change and finding the right number of appropriately qualified staff. It is not hard to understand why an ill-defined, loose desktop strategy makes life a great deal more difficult across the divide between IT and the business – and indeed contributes to that divide in the first place.

STANDARDS

"Users should be given only the tools they need to do the job," says the leading IT analyst firm, Bloor Research. "Ruthless standard-isation is the most effective method of controlling desktop costs," reckons another research company, the OTR Group.

If there is one word that sums up the key to a desktop strategy it is standardisation. The benefits of setting and conforming to standards can be summed up as:

■ *Reduced costs;*

■ *Reduced complexity;*

■ *Reduced lead times for projects;*

■ *Increased control; and*

■ *Improved management.*

Companies that do not first define a standard environment for their desktops – and that means the operating systems, the applications, the hardware, the network and so on – risk undermining the whole of their IT planning.

Organisations that have adopted a strict standardisation of their desktop IT experience faster roll-out times of new systems and are the most successful at cutting costs. Take the example of a leading financial trading firm that relocated to a new building. Instead of taking an existing mixed bag of "non-standard" PCs and applications to the new site, the company wiped the slate clean. As a result, a massive £700,000 was eliminated from an annual maintenance bill of £1.2m for the same number of desktop positions.

CONTROLLING COSTS

If getting costs under control is a primary aim, standardisation is a key action. Analyses of desktop costs consistently show the various elements of support activities, such as running a help desk, as the biggest part of the overall desktop equation.

"Ruthless standardisation" reduces the complexity of the system and therefore reduces support costs. An OTR Group survey found that organisations perceived standardisation to be well ahead of the next most effective cost-reduction techniques, which are deploying system-management tools and consolidating server platforms in distributed environments, as highlighted in the table below.

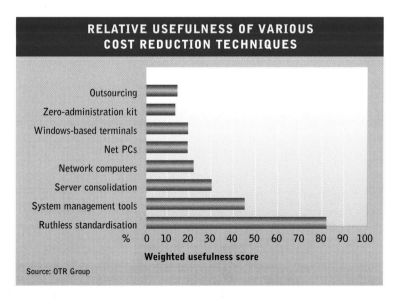

RELATIVE USEFULNESS OF VARIOUS COST REDUCTION TECHNIQUES

Weighted usefulness score

Source: OTR Group

OTR also notes that a common byproduct of standardisation is the reduced cost of hardware and software. If equipment is bought from fewer suppliers better volume discounts can be secured. A good deal of attention needs to be paid to exactly what standards are set and conformed to. For example, a slight adjustment to the specification of a hardware/software combination can result in a significant cost reduction and at the same time, avoid posing any serious risk to performance quality. From the business perspective, it may also be desirable to consider setting different service levels for different business departments within the organisation.

There is a tendency among some companies with business-critical functions such as a trading floor, to ask support organisations for service-level agreements that relate to the whole business. But departments such as human resources and finance clearly do not require the same degree of up-time as market traders. Organisations will often end up with a company-wide service level agreement that does not suit anyone. It is usually more desirable to cost support according to the business function of each different department.

PEOPLE MATTERS

The barriers to change in organisations often have their roots in the past. The potential for lack of understanding between business and IT managers that was discussed earlier has cut both ways. The authors of a Bloor Research report on network computing make this clear. After tracing the flexibility that the PC has brought to users they note: "The second factor is the legacy of how users were treated by IT departments before the advent of PCs. The length of time departments waited for their applications to be developed, the excuses given when systems crashed and the general way in which the IT tail wagged the corporate dog have not been forgotten."

IT literate people with the appropriate understanding of business drivers are often found among internal staff but are commonly deployed doing lower level support work. They are also not exposed to the range of experiences that staff from a specialist provider gain as they move around various businesses.

When it comes to relationships between companies, their users and IT service providers the operative word as we move towards the millennium is partnership. As Bloor Research says: "IT people need to demonstrate a level of corporate maturity to their end users – to show that it is 'safe' in their hands and that a return to centralisation does not mean a return to queueing for its services and dictatorial control."

To help, IT managers may need to re-evaluate the relationships they have with suppliers and consultants. At the moment, few service providers are both independent of desktop suppliers and able to demonstrate the right degree of understanding of technical and business issues. But the concept of the "virtual partnership team", though immature, is taking shape.

User organisations should be able to choose a software vendor, infrastructure vendor and a consultancy firm and put them together to form a solution. This kind of alliance should deliver the best performance: the success of desktop, client/server systems rests on the ability to pick the "best of breed" products and the "best of breed" suppliers.

There is some confusion in the market but the signs are that the right kind of alliances are developing.

THE BUYING PROCESS

Organisations should consider streamlining the tendering process as part of the overall desktop strategy. There is a tendency for those running desktop projects to ask for too much detail in an invitation to tender and take a long time to arrive at a shortlist. (See the next two chapters.) Given that companies with the necessary desktop expertise can be identified fairly easily, it should be possible to draw up a shortlist before going into too much detail and possibly delaying that critical "time to desk" delivery.

Agencies that specialise in external tendering, which promises cost savings, are growing in number. They do, however, have their disadvantages: they often base their service on the contract value alone and not on the long-term costs of the buying decision (where cost of ownership issues can become important).

THE TECHNOLOGY

It is the purpose of this Director's Guide to discuss the effective procurement, deployment and management of desktop systems, not the technology involved. But there are key trends that need to be noted. The primary debate concerns so-called "thin-client" technology, an umbrella term that covers a range of computing desktop devices such as Web browser terminals.

Essentially, the thin-client approach is about simplification, with machines running on central servers. The OTR Group says that its theoretical virtues are very clear and that organisations that have introduced the technologies on a large scale have achieved significant benefits. These include:

■ *Fewer demands on the help desk;*

■ *Lower maintenance costs per desktop; and*

■ *Improved integrity of transaction processing if a terminal fails.*

However, OTR says migration to thin-client technologies will be slow because of users' reluctance – or inability – to move away from PCs (some people do need personal computers to carry out their work) and a lack of confidence in the maturity of the technologies.

Another trend is the increased use of mobile computing, with powerful personal digital assistants (PDAs) such as sophisticated electronic organisers becoming much more widespread. "At least 25 per cent of office workers who normally use PCs will replace them with PDAs," reckons OTR.

Whatever technologies emerge strongest, a key to "future-proof" decision making will be paying close attention to the network. Installing the maximum bandwidth that can be afforded is a move that can hardly be faulted.

KEY POINTS

- A well-designed desktop strategy tackles the twin aims of reducing desktop costs and laying the foundation for fast and cost-effective roll-out of new systems.

- The diversity of environments among organisations makes it difficult to make general statements about particular technologies.

- Few organisations have accurate measures of the true cost of their desktop systems.

- Cultural issues surrounding end-user departments and IT departments need to be addressed by senior management.

- Support costs account for the lion's share of the total cost of ownership of desktop systems for most organisations.

- Standardisation of the desktop is by far the most effective way of gaining control and reducing costs.

- So-called "thin-client" systems have benefits for large organisations, but do not provide the answer for all environments.

- True partnerships with "best of breed" suppliers should be a goal.

FOOTNOTES

How do you control the cost of information systems on the desktop? – OTR Group 1998.

Contact: www.otr.co.uk/aboutotr.htm.

Total Cost of Ownership: Beyond the Hype – Computacenter/Spikes Cavell.

Contact: www.computacenter.com.

The Realities of Network Computing – Bloor Research.

Contact: www.bloor.co.uk.

In today's demanding IT environments, power is vital. But power is nothing without the planning and foresight to make it happen.

That's why hundreds of organisations, both public and private, choose Computacenter – to harness the power of Sun Microsystems™ powerful UNIX systems including Workstations, Servers and Storage.

At Computacenter we turn these IT systems into planned, integrated and managed solutions. Computacenter is Europe's leading distributed IT systems and services company; we have the skills, the partnerships and over 300 staff dedicated to designing, evaluating and testing the distributed information system you need to run your business.

For more information about Computacenter's planning and other services for Sun, please call **0800 7315858**, or visit www.computacenter.com/sun

VALUE ADDED RESELLER
Enterprise Computing Certified

I05265

Chapter 2

Selecting your supplier

PART ONE: TENDERS AND CONTRACTS

Choosing the company that will provide your system is like choosing a spouse – make a mistake and you could be in serious trouble. Annie Gurton, business and technology writer, offers a step-by-step guide to getting it right

The selection of the right supplier is more of a science than an art. Although some degree of subjective judgment is involved, and personal relationships matter, the selection process should be based on a proven methodology that assesses prospective suppliers against a known set of requirements. You should drive the selection process, not allow it or the candidates to drive you. Start by having a clear list of questions and know the answers you are looking for. Choosing the right supplier is like selecting a marriage partner – get it wrong and you can find yourself in a long and painful divorce. Selection criteria should include:

■ *Experience: look for a team with full knowledge of the hardware and software used in your particular market;*

■ *Size and location: make sure the supplier has the range of expertise needed for your project and is accessible – otherwise, you will not be confident that it will manage the project roll-out properly;*

■ *Reputation: place a premium on companies with good names and a good set of reference sites. Ask other companies in your sector who they would recommend (and, equally important, who they would avoid). Look for a loyal and established customer base.*

■ *Leadership: find a supplier with a project manager who you can trust to integrate new and existing systems without impairing business continuity;*

■ *Communications: a good cultural fit with your organisation should mean that interpersonal or technical problems do not become irreconcilable differences;*

■ *Flexibility: your needs may change or new technology may make your original spec out of date. You need a supplier who is close enough to leading manufacturers to deliver a cutting-edge solution that will enable your business to establish and maintain a competitive advantage.*

THE TENDER

The first step when choosing a supplier should be to create a tender document, outlining your requirements, your budget and your timescale. A definition of your company and its business, and the threats and opportunities it faces, will also be useful to suppliers. In addition, you will need to make clear whether you want any services – help with implementation, training, support and long-term maintenance, for example – as well as the basic hardware and software.

The creation of a formal business partnership is of paramount importance. By discussing and agreeing as much as possible with the potential supplier in advance, misunderstandings and false expectations can be avoided. The table at the end of this chapter (page 24) lists the key information you should ask a prospective supplier to provide. Armed with this information, the business is immediately in a better position to evaluate each prospective supplier.

Remember that your requirements are likely to extend beyond the basic hardware and software to installation; systems and network design and subsequent project management; user training and support; re-engineering; diagnostics; and repair and maintenance of your new equipment.

While the company is going to need a supplier or group of

suppliers that can provide all those elements, bear in mind that the more suppliers you have, the greater the cost. The objective is to have as small a number as possible, with each one being the "best-of-breed" in its class or category – for example, application development.

You also need to be clear which skills you have inhouse and which you need to bring in. It may be that you already have programmers and integrators and only need the products and the barest minimum of consultancy and support. Alternatively, you may have virtually no skills inhouse – in which case, your primary task will be to manage the suppliers, not the IT.

MANUFACTURERS OR THIRD-PARTY VENDORS?

The business will need to decide whether it wants to buy direct from a PC vendor or through a third party. There are pros and cons on both sides. Buying products direct may appear cheaper but it means that you will have to deal with several suppliers (sometimes ten or more) and that you will need to take on the responsibility for ultimate integration and project management.

By buying via an established IT systems and services company, however, the organisation can off-load much of that responsibility to one prime contractor or supplier, although it will still have to manage its relationship with its chosen company.

Many direct suppliers these days also provide consultancy and support, training and integration services. Even so, they are rarely a "one-stop-shop" that will take complete charge of your IT requirements. An independent service provider is far more likely to take a business-led approach and understand better the importance of being familiar with your business and your market sector. A direct vendor is invariably product-led while a full services reseller is independent and often better placed to become a closer partner, complementing the work of your in-house IT department.

Depending on the skills within your business, you should consider the input your systems partner needs to make. Many companies take a technology-led approach and this demands that you have clearly defined what the technology must deliver for the underlying business processes.

Some integrators adopt a more strategic approach whereby they look to achieve business improvement through technology – a very different attitude, but an important consideration to make in your choice of a partner.

Whichever type of supplier you believe is better for your organisation, you should be looking primarily for technical competence, on-time delivery and value for money, balanced with a full understanding of your business. Without these attributes, relations can quickly become difficult.

DRAWING UP THE CONTRACT

Spending time at the outset detailing and discussing the contract and making clear your expectations of the project can avoid much acrimony later. What, for example, will happen if the project runs behind schedule, or business is disrupted, or the final system does not deliver to your interpretation of the spec? Milestones, penalties, deliverables and warranties – as well as payment timetables – need to be set down clearly in writing.

Before the contract is signed hold several meetings with the principals and the individuals you will be working with to talk through these issues and to make sure that everyone is working to the same goal and the same standards. Detail a procedure for conflict resolution in the contract and make sure that if the new system does not deliver or fails you will not be left without any IT or with corrupted data.

Some suppliers offer contracts and charges based not only on the actual cost of the hardware and software plus consultancy fees but also on a "value-add" reward that recognises their contribution to a business's success. If, for example, profits soar above a certain point as a direct result of the IT that is introduced, the supplier receives a bonus. Such an arrangement can concentrate a company's mind on helping your business achieve maximum benefit from the project.

TREATING CUSTOMERS AS PARTNERS

The best suppliers treat their customers as partners from the outset. This means being frank about potential problems and about how technologies that are still in the development stage will be brought into the picture. For example, it may be that there is a new operating system, as yet unlaunched and unproven, which may turn out to be better than the current version or existing alternatives. A good supplier will make known its view of the new technology and discuss its implications for your business, including the cost of introducing it at a later stage and even of replacing the system it is currently recommending.

A good supplier will also openly pass on all information about its own suppliers, making it clear, for example, if a merger is being mooted that will affect the long-term support of products on the market today.

It is important, too, to realise that a good supplier/customer relationship is a two-way process and that the supplier will be looking for indications of commitment from you also. For a successful selection process, the candidates will need reassurance that, once contracts are signed, you are not going to become difficult or continue to talk to other prospective suppliers.

No reputable supplier is going knowingly to take on the customer from hell, so you need to convince them that you are going to stick to the agreements once the ink is dry.

MAINTAINING TRUST

When you have a contract, you should not continue to negotiate with other suppliers until such time as the contract is due for renewal. Dalliance with competitors can be very counter-productive when trying to build a strong partnership based on trust. Because of the cost involved, a contract should typically last a number of years – particularly if it is an outsourcing contract, which needs more time to deliver returns on the initial investment.

Once trust does develop, you should let your appointed supplier's staff develop close peer-to-peer relationships with your employees. The supplier is likely to have a wealth of experience. Why not let it use it, for the benefit of your employees and, ultimately, your customers?

The metaphor of a marriage is used a lot to describe the selection of suppliers and relationships with them. The partnership should be about working shoulder-to-shoulder and maintaining open communication. When it is working well life is good. Equally, when it breaks down things turn ugly. It is therefore importance to get the original selection right and tackle difficulties or fears the moment they arise. Ultimately, you should seek a supplier that invests in its customers and takes a long-term view, proven by its track record.

WHAT A POTENTIAL SUPPLIER SHOULD PROVIDE

1 An overview of its business and origins, including its organisational structure, skills, mission and objectives, and recent and proposed changes. Details of directors and key staff and its core business;

2 Evidence of financial stability with three years' audited accounts and projected turnover for the current financial year;

3 A copy of its standard business terms and conditions;

4 A statement of its market position by volume and turnover and the names of its competitors;

5 An outline of its understanding of your business and its objectives and challenges;

6 Details of its customer base, with reference sites that you can contact. An outline of the benefits that it can deliver to each customer and how these are measured;

7 An indication of how much it invests in the development of new products and services and in training. Proof of its commitment to best practice and to building good manufacturer and customer relationships;

8 A description of its disaster recovery and contingency planning;

9 Evidence of its commitment to ISO 9000, TQM policies or any other recognised approval schemes;

WHAT A POTENTIAL SUPPLIER SHOULD PROVIDE

10 A description of its appropriate service agreement and a demonstration of its effectiveness at a reference site; an outline of what its response to technical problems with your system will be;

11 Confirmation of who will manage your account and clarification of the assurances it can give that there will be no change of personnel for the duration of the contract;

12 A declaration of its preferred manufacturers and suppliers and details of the history of its relationship and current spend with each. A statement of the value of those relationships to both it and its customers;

13 Details of the system it intends to provide for you, with explanations of why it will increase your competitive advantage and help ensure your long-term success in your market;

14 An outline of its own use of technology. Does it offer an integrated electronic procurement and tracking system that can be demonstrably integrated into your own internal systems? Does it have an intranet or an extranet? Details of its Web site;

15 A description of its installation process and how it intends to implement the new system for you. Would it want to run a pilot, for example, or go for a big-bang approach? What timescale would it commit to? What would be the project's milestones, and what remedial action would be taken if they were not reached on schedule? How would it manage the transition from your current suppliers?

16 Clarification of how it would measure and review the operational, strategic and tactical benefits that your organisation derives from the contract. How frequently would it carry out a review, and what would its response be if the benefits fell short of the yardsticks used?

17 An outline of its support infrastructure and available skills. What kind of help can it provide?

18 A description of its arrangements for training. Would it subcontract, and if so, to whom? How would it ensure that training was adequate and suitable? Can it provide bespoke training? What about Web-based training?

19 Details of its support, maintenance and warranty options. Would support be subcontracted and, if so, to whom? How would it ensure the level of support is good?

20 Details of its other services and consultancy skills;

21 An explanation of the importance of your business to it;

22 Demonstration of how it can align its services to deliver specific benefits to its customers, matching their business drivers.

SIEMENS

We at Siemens are convinced that in no more than a decade the current conception of the separate worlds of communications and information technology will have been relegated to history.

To fully exploit the convergence of technologies, Siemens have brought together its IT and communications businesses in a single unit. Siemens is now able to offer the entire spectrum of all communication and information products and services from a single source.

As part of this new organisation, Siemens have formed a new organisation that can meet all your information technology requirements. Siemens Computer Systems entire product range is designed to provide competitive advantage by enabling organisations to integrate these two powerful technologies.

So to find out more about Siemens Computer Systems to help your company, whatever your requirements, from compact notebook PCs through home and professional desktops, to workstations, servers and large mainframes, call *0800 125 555 and visit www.siemens.com/servers.*

Siemens Computer Systems
Information meets Communication

Ref: IoD YB

Chapter 3

Selecting your supplier

PART TWO: ASSESSMENT AND DECISION-MAKING

How do you make sure that you judge potential suppliers by the right criteria and win company-wide approval for your choice? Much, says Nick Langley, technology writer, depends on good communication

To a large extent, the process of evaluating potential suppliers is only as good as the invitation to tender documents (ITTs) that have been sent to them. There are a number of important principles to bear in mind. If the ITT has not been drawn up in association with all the relevant departments in your company you will have been unable to establish your priorities and, therefore, the yardsticks against which suppliers are to be judged.

You need to be clear about all the departments' needs and the importance of each of the business processes and services involved: only then can you decide what weight selection criteria should carry. Remember, also, to invite a tender from your existing desktop management services supplier, internal or external. The response of a "known quantity" will provide a further benchmark for assessing potential candidates.

STANDARDISING THE CORE CRITERIA

The ITT should lay down a well-defined procedure for putting forward proposals that all tendering companies should follow. If it does not, you will find it difficult to make direct comparisons between responses and apply your weighting system. You should make it clear that if companies do not use your "standard" procedure, their responses will not be considered.

Over-elaboration should be avoided as much as over-simplification. Just as some client companies include crude tick-lists in their ITT to which all potential suppliers respond to in the affirmative, others spend a great deal of time preparing "model" answers that no candidate can possibly match. Rigid ideals can make a costly and time-wasting second round of tendering necessary. They also rule out potentially better solutions that the team preparing the ITT has not considered.

BE CLEAR ABOUT WHAT IS RELEVANT

Badly prepared ITTs also include questions that don't need to be asked – for example, those covering features or services that all suppliers will offer. By leaving obvious questions out, you will save the supplier's time and your own.

Somehow or other, the costs incurred by the supplier during the tendering process are going to be passed on to the customer, so it is in your interests to keep them down. Concentrate on the real differentiating factors and potential benefits of the proposed solutions. The more detail there is to wade through, the harder it will be to keep the big picture in view.

According to the Business and Accounting Software Developers Association (BASDA), some organisations that send out excessively detailed ITTs complain that many vendors fail to respond. "In a recent selection, one large organisation complained that out of ten ITTs, only two developers had responded, and those put forward inappropriate solutions. One leading European software developer replied that it would cost over £50,000 to respond to that ITT and it was so busy that it could not allocate those resources into a speculative project where it was not even shortlisted," the association says.

Those heavyweight ITTs may not even be asking the right questions. "Organisations and consultants need to move away from tick-lists and feature functions and start looking more closely at the credibility of the vendor, its relationship with its customers and its ability to provide a solution that delivers long-term business benefits," says BASDA.

The previous chapter gives a guide to writing a tender document, but to sum up you should:

■   *Be clear about your priorities – know your "must haves";*

■   *Ask "open" questions;*

■   *Omit non-essential details;*

■   *Try to achieve consistency in the way suppliers respond;*

■   *Avoid rigid preconceptions – leave room for the innovative and the unexpected.*

COMPILING A SHORTLIST

A recent Tate Bramald report into financial software purchasing provides sobering lessons for anyone involved in selecting a supplier through the tendering process. Tate Bramald found that three-quarters of customers were including up to eight suppliers on their shortlists and that half expected the selection process to take more than six months. Extended sales cycles involve extra costs for both vendor and customer.

Having a lengthy shortlist does not necessarily mean you are doing a good job of analysing the market. "If anything, it probably leads to more arbitrary decisions being made," says the marketing manager of one financial software company. "If you're trying to understand the propositions of eight different suppliers, in terms of application solution, technical solution and the viability and reliability of the vendor, I don't believe you'll get all the information you need. If you have just two or three shortlisted you can deal with them at a more detailed level."

A long selection process can leave less time for later phases of the project. "We're seeing less well-executed, more hurried implementations," the marketing manager adds. "There's a protracted sales cycle, then the customer wants it done tomorrow." In a seller's market suppliers may decide to turn contracts that make unreasonable demands down, leaving customers with the very vendors they had tried to weed out.

MATCHING RESPONSES AND COMPANY CULTURE

As chapter 2 makes clear, the tender document should include questions about how suppliers will support particular business objectives – for example, how their solution will provide the expected return on investment. These questions need to be asked clearly and explicitly, requiring suppliers to back their answers up with evidence from their other customers.

As well as financial and quantitative questions, however, you should look at qualitative or "soft" factors. These include issues such as end-user and customer satisfaction, employee morale and motivation, and the need for user training and support. You must also consider how your favoured solution will affect relations between managers and employees, and the degree to which it will influence your ability to carry out strategic planning.

APPROACHES TO SELECTION

There are essentially three ways of evaluating responses:

- *Gut feel: This is what clients are forced to rely on if time is short, or if over-elaborate proposal documents have made it impossible to complete a detailed evaluation within the timescales. This approach is dangerous if used alone, but it should not be discounted. You are unlikely to have a good relationship with a supplier you don't feel comfortable with.*

- *Consultation: As mentioned earlier, talking to all of the departments that will be directly influenced by your decision will help you be clear about what you want and determine your priorities. Providers must be judged, however, not just on their ability to meet your requirements and the quality of their service but also on their flexibility: their solution will have to be adapted as the needs of your business change.*

- *Model answers: This approach not only imposes rigidity but also requires a far more detailed knowledge of the service industry than most clients have.*

RATING THE CANDIDATES

Try to keep your scoring system as simple as possible. Simplest of all is to have three marks – "yes", "no" and "maybe" – for each capability being offered.

That said, the scope and complexity of the required solution must determine the scope and complexity of the method of measuring. You may have a scale of nought to ten where ten means "fully compliant and demonstrably capable of providing the service" and nought "no capability and no intention of developing it". Whatever you do, you need to ensure that the marking scheme is properly documented and unambiguous and thoroughly understood by your assessors.

You should also try to avoid awarding scores for the professionalism of written and oral presentations. This is not a decision in which presentation should triumph over substance. Focus on the ability of candidates to deliver the service you want not their skill at public speaking or designing promotional material.

Once the evaluation is complete but before the decision has been taken, everybody involved in the selection process should meet to discuss their personal responses to the various proposals. It may be that the majority have a positive feeling towards a supplier that has demonstrated its capability to meet requirements but is not top of the ratings. "Soft" factors such as the compatibility of corporate cultures can determine the success of a provider-client relationship. Essentially, the evaluation process has three elements:

■ *Deciding on the evaluation team. Assessors should be drawn from both the business and IT functions. Usually they are broken down into groups, charged with different tasks. You could work on the basis of one candidate per group or ask each group to look at all the responses to one particular section of the tender document. However you divide up the work, consistency of approach is vital. All members of the team must share the same goal, work to the same standards and, as mentioned above, use the same rating system.*

■ *Setting the team to work. As the groups make their assessments, they may need to issue lists of questions in order to clarify certain responses. They will need to do this at the earliest stage possible, to reduce delay.*

■ *Monitoring progress. It's important to make sure the team is not getting lost in the detail. The big picture is what counts.*

INTERNAL AND EXTERNAL COMMUNICATIONS

As part of your preparation for tendering, you will have identified the people from whom you need to seek approval, or ratification of your decision. Well before making the choice, you should prepare the ground by giving reasons why the system or service is to be changed or replaced. You should:

■ *Include not just strategic business factors, but also the operational reasons for the change;*

■ *Get across the likely impact of the change on the way people work;*

■ *Give some idea of the timescales involved;*

■ *Make known how you will communicate your decision.*

You will also need to keep your external business partners up to date with what is going on, insofar as it affects their working relationship with you. If you give suppliers insufficient notice of strategic changes you will inevitably adversely affect your own business as well as theirs.

GETTING BUY-IN FROM THE BOARD

The board may have been involved from the outset, having given its approval for an evaluation of desktop management service providers to take place. In seeking approval for the choice of a particular supplier or service, you should ensure that the proposed solution meets the business case as it was originally presented. You should, of course, include any other business benefits that have emerged during the evaluation.

Your presentation should address the benefits both to the business as a whole and to the areas of responsibility covered by the individual directors.

You should consider communicating your decision jointly with the chosen supplier, which may be able to help with the costs and preparation of the presentation. And you may well find the supplier willing to help with communicating the decision to all levels of the organisation. It is in the supplier's best interest to say why it has been chosen and what it will do. It is likely to have a significant marketing organisation, or it wouldn't have won the business – take advantage of it.

A SELECTOR'S TOP TEN

When choosing a new supplier, rate each prospective candidate 1 to 10 on its:

- Ability to integrate legacy systems with new hardware and new software

- Reliability and dependability

- Skills in areas relevant to you

- Value for money

- Commitment to long-term support using its own resources

- Use of known and established brands

- Loyalty among existing customers

- Fit with your culture

- Relevant previous experience, supported by references from customers

- People, systems and processes that will add value to your business.

CHANGE FOR CHANGE'S SAKE

"If it ain't broke, don't fix it." It may be that you decide that your existing desktop management arrangements fit the company's needs better than any of the external solutions on offer. Your communications both with the board and with employees at every level in the company should allow for this possibility.

KEY POINTS

■ Evaluation criteria need to be established before the ITT is sent out. Tenderers should be asked to respond in a way that allows direct comparison between proposals.

■ Shortlists should be kept short.

■ Weighting or marking systems should be kept as simple as possible.

■ "Soft" factors can be as important for a successful relationship as financial and quantitative criteria. Gut feel should play a part in the selection process.

■ To ensure acceptance of your chosen solution, you should keep everyone affected informed about the reasons for the change, the timescales, and the impact on the way they work.

■ Use your chosen supplier(s) to help you communicate the reasons for any changes, and to outline the plans.

Chapter 4

The art of IT planning

The fast pace of IT product development means thinking ahead is vital. Peter Lorant, services marketing manager at Computacenter, explains how to make sure your needs will be met now and in the future

Richard Branson knows that he needs more than a fleet of immaculate long-haul jets to run his airline – the operation on the ground is supported by sophisticated computer networks. Keeping these networks running well is as important to the efficiency of the airline as the planes are.

At the heart of Virgin's approach is careful planning. It is vital that the company's IT infrastructure keeps pace with the needs of the business. This means focusing on all the elements in the infrastructure and, critically, their inter-relationship.

As Simon Keen, Virgin Atlantic Airways manager of systems and network planning, puts it: "The key thing about a system that is constantly growing is that you can't view it in terms of individual components. You need to be able to look at each element and ensure it is delivering throughout the chain, whether it's an application, server, switch, router, cabling or workstation.

"Our users don't want to know about slow-running networks or outdated software. They want to switch on and be connected wherever they are – at home or in a hotel room on the other side of the world."

WHY PLANNING IS CRITICAL

Planning IT is one of the most complex, yet necessary management activities. Indeed, many of the problems with systems – from failure to deliver business benefits to slow-running applications – derive from poor planning.

Sadly, planning is too often under resourced. Some directors may think they are saving time by passing over it swiftly. In fact, they are probably only storing up problems. A day saved now can create months of extra work if the installed systems do not live up to expectations.

To be effective, planning must make the link between the needs of the business and IT. Obviously, the amount of planning needed varies: a global network of five thousand workstations is in a different league from half a dozen stand-alone PCs. But whatever the new requirement, a good starting point for any company is previous experience.

Before embarking on buying new equipment or planning upgrades it is worth assessing both the reliability and service you have received from existing suppliers. Your review needs to range beyond current performance and ask questions such as:

■ *Do the users feel comfortable with the technology they are using?*

■ *What improvements would they like to see?*

Do not underestimate the value of in-depth feedback from people who are working with IT at the sharp end of the business.

THE RATE OF CHANGE

The next point to consider is that IT continues to change at a breakneck pace. Every day, there is a new announcement that may or may not have relevance to your business. Every few months, the power and functionality of a wide range of PCs and ancillary equipment leap forward. For directors trying to plan for the future, this is confusing.

Large companies can employ teams to monitor trends, with the aid of specialist research organisations such as the Gartner Group and Ovum. Small and medium-sized enterprises do not need to lose out either. One solution is to use an independent systems and services provider which, as part of its service to customers, monitors technology trends and movements in the IT market.

For directors, especially those who are not technically skilled, trying to anticipate the future is a potential minefield. Nonetheless, it is important to understand one central point: new technology used in an effective and creative way delivers genuine competitive advantage and that same technology deployed inappropriately can be wasteful. It is, therefore, necessary both to use the most effective technology and to align it with an appropriate business need.

MAINTAINING STANDARDS

Establishing a standards policy can be highly beneficial in terms of standardising implementation, training and future integration projects.

The issue of standards tends to get brushed aside in IT planning. Most directors know that standards are important, but the way PCs and other equipment is purchased means that they can go by the board. When individuals within departments have authority to buy equipment – and this is the case in most medium to large companies at least – they are often unaware of the standards the company has or simply choose to ignore them.

As an IT infrastructure grows and applications become more interlinked, the lack of standards can create many unexpected problems such as not being able to access information from one database and use it in another application. Of course, having standards is not enough – you also need to police them. This means ensuring that all staff are aware of them and that potential purchases are checked against them before being signed off.

YEAR 2000 COMPLIANCE

There is another issue that needs to be on any current planning agenda – Year 2000 compliance. No business that relies on its PCs and networks can afford to neglect this. This not only means buying new equipment, software and applications that are Year 2000 compliant, but also ensuring existing IT infrastructure will be able to cope with the date change at the start of the new millennium.

THE RIGHT QUESTIONS

The IT director or the director responsible for IT has a critical role to play in planning, but other directors should be involved. They can help the business as a whole lower its IT costs, simply by asking a few more questions. Why do you need this? Is it really going to help the business? The easy questions can often produce some revealing answers.

CHECK UP ON VENDORS

Vendor accreditation is also a critical part of the planning process. Nobody pretends that major brands will go out of business, but the accreditation process does more than tell you whether or not your vendor is likely to stick around.

It is important to be certain that the company you are buying from has reliable products, a good base of users and is investing in the technologies that will support you in the future.

Many companies will buy from far more than two vendors. Indeed, a medium to large company could find itself buying hardware, software and networking products from anything between 100 and 200 vendors.

Checking on them all could prove almost impossible, especially as the big vendors announce new plans and developments almost weekly. There are two possible approaches to vendor accreditation:

- *In-house: If you choose this option you need to focus on the key vendors – those that have the potential to damage your business if they fold – and look at a few critical issues within each one. These could include not just the financial state of health of the companies, but the development and direction of any products that are crucial to your business.*

- *Vendor accreditation programmes: These programmes are carried out by leading third-party resellers of hardware and software. The big players devote substantial resources to this activity. Moreover, because their global purchases for major vendors often run into hundreds of millions of dollars, they carry clout at the highest levels. Thus, they can gain access to product development plans often not disclosed to the ordinary end-user.*

AUDIT WHAT YOU'VE GOT

One big problem with any IT planning process is that few companies know what computers and software they already have. This has been a particular problem at the desktop level, where purchase and installation are decentralised.

Year 2000 compliance programmes have made many companies draw up an accurate inventory of their desktop IT. But auditing the desktop should not be a one-off activity. In a company of any size, the inventory is bound to be out of date within a couple of weeks and seriously inaccurate inside a year. This means there is a need for an ongoing management procedure that keeps track of what IT infrastructure exists – and where it is.

An accurate audit of systems is not an optional extra. Existing systems may make it difficult or even impossible to install new hardware or software. Keeping up to date is not the only benefit of a desktop audit. Other potential benefits include:

■ *The discovery of equipment that your help desk did not know about. This means the help desk can then gear up to support that equipment.*

■ *The discovery of equipment that was not covered by any maintenance agreements. Alternatively, you may find that equipment listed on maintenance contracts no longer exists. Either way, there are opportunities to improve service or cut costs.*

HELPING YOUR SUPPLIER TO HELP YOU

"Business take-on" and "transition management" may sound suspiciously like pieces of consultant-speak but they relate to important issues that can help ensure new IT systems meet your expectations and fulfil their potential.

User-dissatisfaction is a problem that has dogged desktop IT since it emerged in the eighties. Of course, extravagant promises from vendors are partly to blame, but users must also bear some of the responsibility: too often, they have not made their expectations of a new system completely clear. They need, for example, to state:

■ *What volume of work do they expect to be carried out;*

■ *What response times they expect on screen; and?*

■ *How quickly they expect back-up support to be provided.*

Those planning the parameters of the solution should also produce a clear model of what users want from the system. This should then be discussed with a selection of users to agree what is possible so that targets can be set with them and the supplier accordingly.

FINANCING THE INVESTMENT

The economics of IT investment is a weighty topic in its own right. Calculations become increasingly complex as issues such as the residual value of the equipment and improvements in productivity are included. However, there are some key issues. Principal among these is the buy-versus-lease decision. Many companies have it ingrained in their culture that they need to own their equipment. The computers become an asset on the books and attract tax relief. But leasing could become more popular for two reasons:

■ *The first is the increasing need to look more closely at how capital is used. As the economy slows down, some companies may prove reluctant to buy IT.*

■ *The second is the increasing need for flexibility. Those companies that are "power users" of computers – for example, finance houses, graphics and design houses and IT businesses themselves – want to upgrade with ever increasing frequency. The merchant bank Barclays Capital "refreshes" its equipment base every 15 months. It is possible to draw up a lease that accommodates this kind of change.*

Whichever method of financing you choose, there is one essential factor to consider: total cost of ownership (TCO). This not only includes the original purchase price, but costs such as help desks, maintenance, and so on over the lifetime of the equipment. According to one study, the original purchase price may represent only 21 per cent of the TCO.

THE NEED FOR TECHNICAL HAND HOLDING

The largest organisations may have enough technical expertise to manage their desktop IT in-house. The smallest may find their needs can be handled by a reasonably technically literate member of staff. But those in the middle – the vast majority of companies – may feel the need for technical hand holding.

In any project involving hardware and software from different vendors this can be a major concern – especially if problems arise over interaction between different products. It is another argument for buying from an independent systems services provider with suitable resources that can take a holistic view of the whole project and be responsible for ensuring that everything runs smoothly.

KEY POINTS

- Make planning the first step in any desktop IT project.

- Quantify the business goals that the solution should help deliver.

- Work towards making the standards of different parts of desktop IT converge.

- Check potential vendors for financial stability, satisfied users and relevant product development plans.

- Audit existing systems to gain a true picture of your project's starting point.

- Provide useful relevant information to a trusted supplier, whether manufacturer or reseller.

- Explore different ways to finance the project.

Who's at the hub of today's most important strategic IT partnerships?

We are. And whether it's working with technology partners, channel partners, or our customers, it's a true collaboration in which we help innovate, develop and fine-tune the best solutions – in everything from Internet commerce to mission- **COMPAQ** critical applications in finance, communications, manufacturing and beyond

Better answers.

www.compaq.co.uk

Chapter 5

Getting the right kit

The vast array of hardware and software can make life baffling for the IT buyer. Peter Bartram, business writer, highlights potential procurement pitfalls – and how to avoid them

If you have bought any PCs recently, you may be able to identify with Kelvin Allen, technical infrastructure manager for Zurich Insurance, one of the world's top ten insurance companies. "A large number of PC equipment and software manufacturers seem to have a supermarket mentality," Allen says. "They will sell you the kit – and lots of it – but getting any really deep support is extremely difficult."

Allen's comments highlight one of the problems that businesses face when investing in desktop IT. Many vendors still focus on "shifting boxes": they are not too interested in whether the "boxes" they sell are the right ones for the buyer or fit in with a company's overall IT strategy.

For Zurich Insurance the solution was to buy its desktop IT through a third-party supplier that offered consultancy and maintenance and support services. Whether or not companies opt for the same route, there is a range of issues that they need to consider when setting out to procure desktop IT.

MANAGING THE TECHNOLOGY LIFECYCLE

Buying desktop IT is significantly different from purchasing other types of office equipment. This is principally because the purchase has to been seen in the context of a technology lifecycle. The PCs you choose today may have to link into existing and future networks, may need to be upgraded later and may, ultimately, be replaced by new but compatible equipment. The decision you take now has far-reaching implications. You need to be sure that the vendor you choose is likely to develop its product range in ways that will meet the future needs of the business.

Understanding product lifecycles is not easy and for some companies this strengthens the case for buying from third-party resellers which monitor product developments carefully – rather than from manufacturers directly.

The task of the buyer is complicated further by there being a bewildering choice of hardware and software, despite the dominance of just a few big names. Even within one leading manufacturer such as IBM there is a whole range of desktop PC brands, networking products and printing technologies. Making the right choice is not easy, but a determined effort to identify the most appropriate products pays dividends in the long run.

Another issue worth noting is the expense of shopping around for IT. One bank calculated that it cost about £140 just to raise a purchase order for a new PC or piece of software when staff time was taken into account. This means there is a real value in taking a long hard look at your IT procurement process and the costs associated with it.

DEVELOPING TRUE SUPPLIER PARTNERSHIPS

In order to manage product lifecycles to best effect companies need to develop a long-term relationship with desktop IT suppliers. There are two main approaches to building this relationship:

■ *The first is to buy from one main supplier. By focusing on one manufacturer's product lines, it is simpler to monitor developments. Depending on the size of your business, you can become a valued client. In the case of the larger manufacturers, you can also source a range of ancillary products and support services. Also, you may be in a position to drive a tough bargain on price – again depending on the size of your business and its strategic value to the manufacturer.*

- *The second approach is to choose a third-party supplier that will help you source products from across a number of vendors' product ranges. This means you can select from a wider range of products and get third-party guidance.*

Whichever route you choose, there are some key points about developing an effective partnership:

- *There should be a good cultural fit between your company and the supplier. You need to feel that the values that drive decision making in your supplier's organisation are in harmony with your way of doing business.*

- *You need to be sure you can trust your partner and be confident that he or she has your best interests at heart and is providing best advice.*

- *Your IT partner and your own staff must communicate well. Depending on the size of your business, this may mean your supplier providing a dedicated account manager. At the very least, there should be a single point of contact – someone who understands your business and the details of the relationship. It is important to remember that communication is a two-way process. The supplier will be able to help you more effectively if it fully understands your plans.*

- *Your partner should provide considerable assistance with managing your desktop IT portfolio. It should help you work according to your business's needs and priorities. It is no good, for example, having expensive and powerful but under-used PCs in one area while lacking power in another.*

Choosing the right desktop services partner who is a third-party reseller will ensure that you gain an independent intermediary between yourself and the manufacturers. This allows you to review your options comparatively with another expert opinion and should aid decision making considerably.

By working closely with you to develop a clear set of criteria about how the kit will be used, your desktop services partner can offer you a wider and more flexible portfolio of equipment for your people to choose from, while still maintaining adherence to your technical standard. For example, when the National Westminster Bank wanted to invest in laptop computers for staff training, it called on its third-party supplier

CASE STUDY

THIRD-PARTY CHEMISTRY

When Boots the Chemist decided to upgrade its desktop IT system it turned to a third-party reseller to help with procurement.

It wanted to migrate from Windows 95 to Windows NT and incorporate Lotus SmartSuite as a standard desktop application. More power, more memory, improved system management and better local-area network communication were also priorities.

As the project gathered pace, Chris Edwards, the infrastructure projects manager for information systems at Boots, realised that his staff were spending more time dealing with upgrades or replacements and less time on value-added work such as technical and software development. Edwards decided to hire an independent systems and services provider to organise PC procurement and delivery, thus freeing up the members of his team to make better use of their skills.

Explains Edwards: "The task goes a lot further than just supplying a pre-configured PC. The real value to us lies in having somebody to deal with all the peripheral issues which surround a new desktop. We need someone who can manage all the relationships both externally and internally and be capable of using their initiative to get the job completed quickly."

A member of Boots staff kicks off the procurement process by placing an order with the internal purchasing department, which, in turn, passes it to the IT partner. The order is for one of a previously agreed set of configurations. From there, the IT partner takes over, arranging everything needed to ensure the PC is ordered and delivered.

Edwards sees this process working well in the company's "get on and do it culture". Underlining the importance of trust in an effective partnership, he points out that Boots' IT provider is free to use its own judgment if a particular installation costs more than the budget.

"We have an agreement that both defines those parts of the process that are our responsibility and gives our supplier the freedom to achieve its tasks without constantly coming back for approval," he says.

to advise on the options. It was given information about laptops that were proven and reliable, could provide a CD-Rom drive and offer "future proofing" through memory expansion and optional modem. The supplier then arranged demonstrations of the top two laptops on the shortlist.

UNDERSTANDING VENDORS' PLANS

Managing the products in your desktop IT portfolio is, of course, closely linked to "supplier management". You need to fully understand how major vendors, such as Microsoft in operating systems or SAP in databases, plan to develop their products in the future. Only then can you decide which upgrades your business will require.

The development of Microsoft's Windows operating system illustrates this point. Many businesses started with version 3.1. Then Microsoft announced Windows 95 and later Windows 98. However, not all companies decided to switch immediately to 95. Some preferred to wait for 98. Others are still switching to 95, even though 98 is available. Still others are waiting for Microsoft's next announcement.

Leading hardware and software products pass through so many development stages that it is virtually impossible for any user to upgrade step by step to every version. The key aspect of supplier management from the users' point of view is to understand the milestones in a product's development – for example, version 3.11 of Microsoft's Windows.

At the same time, the user needs to pull out from the mass of development detail those technical features that could open up new opportunities for it. For example, Windows 98's ability to link desktop computing with Internet access more effectively could be highly significant for some businesses.

As dominant players emerge in most areas of software and hardware the task of supplier management might become slightly easier: there will simply be fewer credible companies around, fewer companies to track. However, the pace of product development is likely to quicken as the market leaders fight to retain their positions.

CASE STUDY

BANKING ON E-COMMERCE

E-commerce is making it easier to shop for desktop IT, reducing the cost of procurement and cutting down on paperwork. But perhaps its greatest benefit is quick access to information both before and after orders are made.

Niels Olsen, head of Internet/intranet Development at Greenwich Natwest, an investment banking subsidiary of NatWest Bank plc, believes that online procurement is the quickest way of ordering and receiving products and services at the lowest cost to internal business units. For Greenwich Natwest this is key, as without these solutions the business suffers.

Greenwich Natwest originally had a manual procurement process which involved lengthy processing, from initial order to the purchase requisition.

"By the time the order arrived at the purchasing department to push the order through to the supplier, the product pricing might be outdated or even out of stock," explains Olsen. "Moving this process online and making it accessible via our corporate intranet gives us immediate access to stock information.

"We can also gain authorisation much more quickly and track the progress of the order. This means that our business gets faster turnaround of orders and we save money on internal administration and resource."

FINDING WHAT YOU NEED

Some directors have been surprised to discover that it is not always possible to obtain the hardware and software they need within the short time-frames of so many desktop IT projects.

Finding equipment that meets the often very precise specifications of a brief can be difficult. In addition, all vendors prefer to keep stockholding to a minimum. When you start on a new desktop IT project, therefore, it is important to check that the equipment you need will be available by the time you need it. Do not assume that the supplier you want to use will automatically be able to provide it.

This supply-and-demand problem highlights the danger of ad hoc IT planning. Managers develop a new business need and demand a system to meet it – yesterday. Looking ahead helps to predict likely needs and avoids the last-minute panic of trying to locate hard-to-find equipment. (See previous chapter for a guide to planning.) As well as generating panic, the ad hoc approach can increase costs. The user has less room to negotiate on price if the vendor knows that he or she needs the equipment within days. The appropriate kit may have to be sourced from abroad – further adding to costs.

Suppliers do recognise there is an availability problem and are trying to improve turnaround in response to customer demand. For example, Computacenter has been working with IBM and more recently Hewlett Packard on channel assembly programmes. Whereas previously IBM supplied its computers fully built to Computacenter, it now despatches main components as base unit "shells". The shells comprise the motherboard and processor allowing Computacenter to configure additional hardware and software for each unit to meet the specific needs of individual customers. Devolving the last stage of the building process to Computacenter, enables a far greater range of standard builds to be offered to customers, and shortens the time between order and installation and improves quality. Despite these developments, however, there is no escaping the fact that better forecasting by users will make sourcing both easier and cheaper.

KEY POINTS

- Focus on the technology lifecycle in order to win long-term benefits from desktop IT procurement.

- Look at the relative merits and demerits of using manufacturers and resellers.

- Develop a real partnership with your main supplier or suppliers.

- Manage your desktop IT portfolio as an integrated whole.

- Understand the vendors' development plans for products at the heart of your desktop IT.

- Plan ahead to avoid last-minute headaches.

- Consider the benefits of developing e-commerce between your company and key suppliers.

Chapter 6

Practice made perfect

Desktop IT plans affect everyone in the office. So it is important they are put into practice carefully. Peter Bartram, business writer, looks at how two companies set about successful implementation

When Business Link London, part of the national network of business advice centres that help small to medium-sized enterprises, wanted to upgrade its desktop IT it knew that the success of the project would lie as much in the thoroughness of the implementation as the quality of the planning.

The organisation's IT manager, Geoff de Metz, knew there were problems with the desktop set-up. "Although we had a technologically sound solution, it did not deliver the efficiency we hoped it would," he says. "For example, there was an unacceptably high level of voicemail tag and duplication of effort."

But de Metz wanted to do more than merely resolve problems. He wanted to lift Business Link London's desktop IT to a new level – a level where it would start to contribute real value to the organisation and where, as a result, it would be seen as an important working tool by all staff.

DISTINGUISHING PRIORITIES FROM PREFERENCES

Of course, there were also technical priorities. "One of our prime requirements was to incorporate e-mail and the ability to access online information. We wanted to make use of Internet technologies, to deal electronically with partners, suppliers and customers and we had to incorporate X.400 capability to comply with DTI requirements. We particularly wanted desktop faxing to make the lives of our staff easier," de Metz explains.

TURNING THEORY INTO PRACTICE

All this sounds good in theory, but can it work in practice? Business Link London decided to divide its project into logical phases. These were:

- *Phase one: providing e-mail and developing an IP addressing strategy – both key to future developments;*

- *Phase two: extending the functions of users' desktops;*

- *Phase three: linking all staff to the Internet for e-mail and browsing.*

Phase one required the company to install a server that would deliver both the e-mail and the X.400 messaging. It made its selection – Compaq ProLiant – on the basis of the total cost of ownership of the equipment (see chapter 4). The next step was to standardise PCs for the desktop – again, total cost of ownership was one of the main selection criteria.

To implement phase two, Business Link London chose to capitalise on what it had in legacy systems – Microsoft Exchange. De Metz explains the background to his decision: "We already had experience with Microsoft Office and our staff were comfortable with it, so when we started to look at additional desktop functionality we leaned towards staying with a successful solution." Now staff can send desktop faxes using Exchange as a gateway.

The third phase was a key productivity need for Business Link London's call centre. A lot of the work involves finding information and sign-posting callers, and the team has to be able to access online information from a wide range of sources. Staff are now able to surf the Web at will.

"We have found that the general comfort level among staff using the technology has been raised very substantially," says de Metz. Business Link London's success was partly due to its decision to work with an independent systems services provider, which brought critical experience to the project and helped overcome problems.

IMPLEMENTING A PAN-EUROPEAN PROJECT

While effective implementation was critical to the success of Business Link London's solution, the issue becomes even more compelling in a pan-european project. In the case of WorldCom International, a provider of communication services for business and government, rapid expansion meant that new PCs, servers and office applications needed to be installed in nine European countries. Terry Downing, international information technology manager, explains: "The company's infrastructure was reaching the point where it was becoming hard-pressed to cope with the way the company had been expanding. There were growing pressures on staff as well as the technologies.

"A variety of systems was in use and this affected staff's ability to share documents and exchange information. We were faced with a choice of expanding the existing infrastructure or taking a clean sheet and building an infrastructure to take us forward. The solution was a common operating environment (COE) for all European offices."

CAREFUL PLANNING IS CRUCIAL

Successful implementation is normally underpinned by careful planning – and the WorldCom project was no exception. Each office undertook an audit of its needs and passed the results to Downing's team.

A schedule was then prepared, pinpointing which PCs would be upgraded and which replaced. Implementation was based on a detailed project plan that was used as a model for each office. The plan included developing a migration path from Novell software to Windows NT and designing a domain that provided the needed security and operational flexibility.

The pattern was the same for each office. Three or four days before a weekend, the third-party supplier flew its project team out. The team started by identifying any personal data or software to make sure it was transferred from the old workstations, before preparing the office for the new equipment. Implementation took place over a weekend so that staff would come in on Monday morning and everything would work when they switched on.

To back up the implementation plan, each user had one-to-one training over the next two days. All equipment had been unpacked, configured and tested before it was sent to the offices. This meant that errors and omissions could be dealt with before work started on site, saving valuable time.

THE VALUE OF GOOD PROJECT MANAGEMENT

The experiences of Business Link London and WorldCom International offer several lessons. The first is the importance of planning. Planning includes not only working out how to deliver what the business needs, but also making sure that the hardware and software selected will meet those needs and, where necessary, work alongside existing equipment.

At the planning stage you should consider that your own business applications will need to run alongside typical desktop applications such as spreadsheets and e-mail. At the end of the day, making applications work effectively often comes down to detailed planning of the minutiae of hardware such as levels of memory, graphics cards and modems. Without this kind of detailed planning, implementation may founder.

The second key lesson is the value of developing a project plan. Often, upgrading desktop IT can seem a troublesome activity that diverts management attention from the business in hand. Yet moving forward without a project plan is a sure-fire way to create more trouble. It is possible that a project involving fewer than, say, ten PCs can manage without a formal plan. Anything involving above that number certainly cannot.

BREAK BIG PROJECTS DOWN INTO PHASES

The experience of Business Link London shows the benefits to be gained from breaking big projects down into phases. Doing this ensures that the resources you have to carry out the project are not over-stretched.

In addition, you can make sure that one implementation phase is working correctly before moving on to the next. Implementing a project in stages need not delay the completion of the whole: in fact, it may mean that everything is up and running effectively more quickly.

ALWAYS REMAIN FLEXIBLE

There are a couple of other general points can be made about successful implementation:

■ *Always be flexible. No matter how carefully desktop IT projects are planned at the outset, it seems that they have an irresistible urge to change shape as they progress. There is always somebody, somewhere who discovers a new feature or function they "must have" once the project implementation is under way. The secret of success is to handle this problem without letting it derail the project plan. There is no reason why changes cannot be incorporated as the implementation proceeds – provided the incorporation is made in an ordered way.*

■ *Nominate somebody to take charge of the project. This is usually the project manager, who will sign off changes to specifications before they are made. Before the project manager agrees to a change, it should be checked against a set of criteria to decide whether it really is a "must have". At the same time, the cost and time implications of making it should be assessed against the project plan.*

IDENTIFYING THE KEY PLAYERS

Most implementations usually involve bringing together two sets of people – the IT professionals and those who will ultimately use the new desktop IT. It pays to identify the "owners" of the business processes that will benefit from the project. Gaining their enthusiastic "buy-in" will certainly help the project to proceed more effectively, especially when it comes to the inevitable disruption – no matter how minimal – that any significant desktop IT project involves.

In fact, projects work best when there is a strong partnership between the IT professionals and those working within the business processes affected. Setting out to foster this partnership is the responsibility of senior managers on both sides.

It is also important to define roles and responsibilities in the implementation process. In-house staff and those working for suppliers and contractors should be equally aware of what is expected of them.

Responsibilities should be spelt out clearly in terms of costs, timescales and deliverables.

Given the extra work that a major desktop IT project involves, it is tempting to outsource as much as possible. But attempting to outsource the whole of a project can be counterproductive. As the Business Link and WorldCom case studies show, working with external partners who understand the business imperatives behind the project as well as the technical issues, greatly increases the chances of success.

ULTIMATE RESPONSIBILITY RESTS IN-HOUSE

In the end, responsibility for successful delivery must rest in-house. If senior managers do not have control over what is happening, there is a strong likelihood that the project will fail.

A final implementation issue needs to be mentioned. Skills shortages seem to have dogged the computer industry since it began. There is a particularly acute shortage of people with the best-quality desktop IT skills at the moment. This is partly because desktop IT is growing so fast and partly due to the rapid pace of change in the industry which can confound even those who work in it. There are simply too few good, up-to-date people to go round.

Shortages will almost certainly become more acute now as more companies start to work on the Year 2000 problem. This means that although the basic prices of hardware will continue to fall, the overall cost of projects could rise sharply – bid up by ever spiralling salary and consultancy costs. This underscores the vital importance of making certain that any project is planned and implemented with considerable care.

KEY POINTS

- Remember that without a sound project plan, implementations stand more chance of failure.

- Break large projects down into phases.

- Bring in people with the technical skills you lack in-house to supplement your project team.

- Focus on integrating legacy applications with any innovations.

- Win the support of process and application owners and forge partnerships between the business and IT specialists.

- Identify the skills needed to complete the project successfully.

Chapter 7

Cutting the cost of user support

Aftercare of your system should not be an afterthought. Annie Gurton, business and technology writer, explains why making support an integral part of IT planning will save time – and money

According to the research company Gartner Group only 21 per cent of the cost of an IT system over three years is accounted for by the purchase of hardware and software. The remaining 79 per cent goes into support and management.

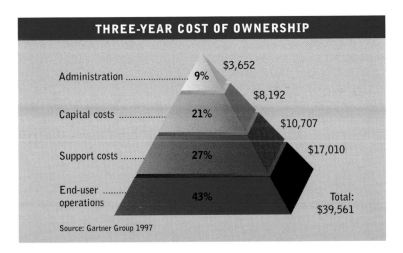

THREE-YEAR COST OF OWNERSHIP

Administration	9%	$3,652
Capital costs	21%	$8,192
		$10,707
Support costs	27%	$17,010
End-user operations	43%	Total: $39,561

Source: Gartner Group 1997

MANAGING THE TOTAL COST OF OWNERSHIP

The case for better planning to reduce the need for system "aftercare" and, therefore, the total cost of ownership (see chapter 4) is strong: all too often, support is seen as an ad hoc extra rather than an integral part of the planning and purchase of a new or upgraded computer system.

If support is not thought about until the time it is required, and no investment is made in support planning, capital costs and the risks that business will be lost invariably increase. Support should be planned like insurance, so that the cost can be predicted and built into budgets at the time of purchase and the damage caused by any problems minimised or prevented.

AVOID PROBLEMS THROUGH PLANNING

Companies that fail to make proper support plans can find that users waste time trying to find the person with the knowledge to help them, systems continue to flounder on, failing to deliver best performance, and disasters cause the temporary collapse of the business. With the right planning, problems are anticipated and therefore resolved more cheaply and more quickly, ensuring that users get the best out of the system and that disruption is kept to a minimum.

It is at the planning and purchase stage that an evaluation of short-term and long-term support and maintenance needs should be made. After that, the quality of support you receive – and its cost-effectiveness – will depend in large part on the quality of your relationship with your supplier. You need to get to know the individuals who will be managing your account, so that they can become familiar with your organisation, its business drivers and its IT needs.

By working together, you can ensure that your system and the users' requirements are aligned and that system and user downtime is reduced to an absolute minimum. In this way, the overall cost of your IT is kept down, the profitability of your business is protected and your competitive edge is developed and sustained into the distant future.

Support can be broken down into several key aspects:

■ *Hardware maintenance and upgrades;*

■ *Software upgrades and user support; and*

■ *Disaster prevention and recovery.*

Although each requires a different solution, an integrated approach is best, particularly if you have bought products from a variety of vendors. You need a support provider that is able to:

■ *Deal with hardware and system problems;*

■ *"Address" software application program faults; and*

■ *Offer an overall IT strategy for business continuity despite any predictable or unavoidable disasters.*

HARDWARE MAINTENANCE AND UPGRADES

All hardware products come with a statutory warranty that protects you in the event of fault or breakdown, but there are surprising variations even between basic statutory agreements. Furthermore, for most organisations, a basic statutory warranty is not enough to deliver adequate support. The answer is to take out an umbrella support agreement that matches your organisation's business requirements, ensuring that your users get the help they need and that machines are upgraded fast enough to sustain business continuity.

Your supplier should offer a support package tailored to the size of your enterprise and the type of business that you run. While most users can manage quite happily on a next-day resolution service others need almost instantaneous support – if a PC goes down an on-site engineer has to be at hand to get it working again within minutes.

Businesses that depend on communication and information need fast, efficient and professional IT support. Next-day service that delivers an engineer to a site, but does not guarantee that he is able to fix any problem straightaway may not be good enough. Some support providers assure you of next-day on-site maintenance, but fail to add that it may be up to a week before they get your IT working productively again; they may have to come back several times before they can fix the problem. You should therefore look for a provider that promises a next-day resolution as well as a next-day service. Engineers should telephone the day a problem is reported so that they can ascertain the nature of the trouble and therefore be sure to take the right replacement parts with them.

SOFTWARE UPGRADES AND USER SUPPORT

From time to time, you will need to have your software upgraded, either because the manufacturers have brought out new versions, or because the demands on your system have changed. You may also need help with application program faults.

Your chosen supplier should be capable of taking control of any system remotely, so that, where at all possible, problems can be diagnosed and fixed without an engineer calling at your premises.

This service is particularly useful for organisations that employ remote workers across a wide geographical spread, but it also saves time and money for those operating from one site. Sophisticated suppliers may be able to upgrade desktops and servers remotely and ensure that all users have the same version of products, depending on the standard of an organisation's IT environment.

Whether they work on-site or from another location, however, engineers should be familiar not only with the vendor's products but also with your system and how it supports your business. You should therefore look for a supplier that ensures all its support staff are continually updated on all new versions and upgrades and that they can upgrade systems competently and reliably, adapting them to deliver optimum performance to users and their organisation.

Of course, optimum performance depends on the competence of end users as well as that of support staff. This is why a programme of user education should be one of the first steps in any support planning. Encouraging employees to understand the business's IT system will ensure that they don't call a support person to handle minor problems – such as the replacement of a printer cartridge - and incur unnecessary costs.

Users have to follow the right procedures if stress placed on the desktop system is to be kept to a minimum. Many faults can be avoided by ensuring that employees "boot up" and close down properly and back up with the recommended frequency.

If users are competent and confident fewer easily solvable problems are reported and less expensive time is wasted. One of the goals of training, therefore, is self-sufficiency. If users can help themselves they will not only save the company money but also get more satisfaction out of the system.

By giving the right kind of information, call centres and help desk users can telephone if they need assistance and can help train staff to deal with problems on their own. Telling staff how to fix problems rather than fixing them for them will reduce their need for a helpline.

OUTSOURCING THE CALL CENTRE OPERATION

Some larger organisations create their own call centres. However, setting up and maintaining a centralised help desk can be costly and can tie up internal staff whose skills would be better used elsewhere. Many business managers therefore choose to outsource all or part of their call centre operation. By handing the running of the call centre to a professional organisation that already has the technology and the staff in place costs are immediately reduced and support becomes quantifiable and controllable.

Larger support companies continually update call centre staff on the wide-ranging systems used by businesses. This means that problems can be dealt with quickly. Call centres should ultimately help you improve the way your system is run. They can do this by:

- *Telling you about the support calls your employees have made;*

- *Helping you to identify users who need more training; or*

- *Highlighting the areas of the system that might need reviewing as a result of data overload or lack of power and memory.*

All IT-dependent organisations should, of course, analyse support requirements themselves and take remedial action where necessary, but they can pinpoint deficiencies far more effectively when the support provider is involved.

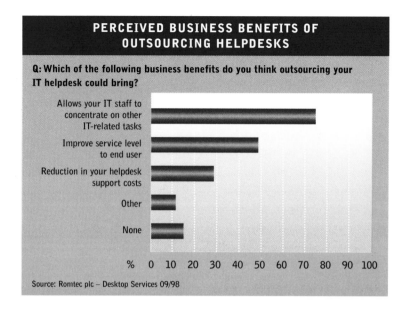

PERCEIVED BUSINESS BENEFITS OF OUTSOURCING HELPDESKS

Q: Which of the following business benefits do you think outsourcing your IT helpdesk could bring?

Allows your IT staff to concentrate on other IT-related tasks

Improve service level to end user

Reduction in your helpdesk support costs

Other

None

%　0　10　20　30　40　50　60　70　80　90　100

Source: Romtec plc – Desktop Services 09/98

DISASTER PREVENTION AND RECOVERY

Statistics show that any business that is unable to trade for more than seven days has more than a 90 per cent risk of collapse. It is essential, therefore, to have a contingency plan for ensuring business continuity in the event of a disaster such as flooding or bombing. You need a supplier that can promise to have your business operating again as quickly as possible.

Unfortunately, many board directors fail to realise the importance of computers and their data until it is too late. Anyone who has suffered the loss of critical IT systems and data integrity will confirm, however, that contingency planning is crucial and should start as soon as the new system has been purchased.

Your supplier should continually monitor your systems and data so that they can be replicated at a new location in the event of the original site being decommissioned.

A reputable support organisation will also be able to recommend and install various security devices, firewalls and encryption products to ensure that your system is not at risk from corporate thieves, cyber-hackers or mischievous ex-employees.

Protecting a system against malicious intruders is a crucial part of modern support services and disaster management.

Prevention is better than cure and it is also possible to get your system protected against interruptions in electricity supply and against accidental damage by incompetent users and software viruses. Taking such preventative action will reduce your ongoing costs and the long-term cost of ownership of your system.

KEY POINTS

■ Seventy nine per cent of the cost of an IT system over three years goes into support and management.

■ Support should be planned and the costs built into your budgets. It is worth involving your chosen supplier at this stage.

■ Secure a support package which is tailored to the size of your enterprise and the type of business that you run.

■ Your chosen supplier should be capable of taking control of any system remotely.

■ Encourage staff to familiarise themselves with the company's system to avoid having to pay out for minor maintenance jobs.

■ Contingency planning is a must.

■ Your supplier should play an active role in improving the way your IT system is run.

■ Develop good relationships with the individuals who will be managing your support account.

BEFORE WE PUT OUR NAME ON THE OUTSIDE,

WE PUT IT WHERE IT REALLY COUNTS.

Real beauty is more than skin deep, that's why we make most of what goes into our computers ourselves - from hard disks to memory chips. It means you know what you're getting: superb quality across the line, from the inside out. You'll often find our name inside PCs wearing other well-known badges. We regard that as a compliment. For more inside information, visit us at www.fujitsu-computers.com.

pentium®II
PROCESSOR

FUJITSU

PCs • NOTEBOOKS • SERVE

Business License Code
SB443

COMPUTACENTER (UK) LIMITED

MARKETING DEPARTMENT

COMPUTACENTER HOUSE

93-101 BLACKFRIARS ROAD

LONDON SE1 8YX

Please tick box

Please arrange for Computacenter to telephone me
to discuss managing my desktop IT □

Please send me a Computacenter brochure □

Name _____

Title _____

Company _____

Address _____

_____

_____ Postcode _____

Telephone _____ E-mail _____

Nature of business _____

Number of computers in organisation: 1-50 □   51-100 □   101-300 □   301-500 □

500-1000 □   Over 1000 □

Chapter 8

Lessons in training

Too little knowledge is a dangerous and expensive thing. Nick Beard, head of training at Computacenter, explains how to ensure your staff gain the maximum from training investment

It is no good investing lots of money in leading-edge technology if the only people who can use it properly are the company's IT department. The fundamentals of how the system works should be understood by everyone who uses it. If they are, the company will be able to cut the cost of user support and, therefore, the overall cost of owning its IT. If they are not, you will waste money, fail to get the best from your system and be unlikely to sustain the competitive advantage IT can deliver.

Of course, the specific training needs of individuals do vary – largely according to the job they do and the software they use – and you should look for a training provider that can demonstrate an understanding of your organisation and your users as well as your system and the hardware and software you have bought. The trainer you choose should have wide experience in the delivery and design of courses and be able to offer skilled trainers at a location to suit you. You may also need it to provide the relevant equipment for "students" to use.

While the human resource or personnel department will usually keep a record of courses that staff have taken, a healthy company also encourages individuals to take some of the responsibility for training. Typically it is employees themselves who have the most complete understanding of the skills they need to do their work. They should be encouraged to seek out training that will help them improve their ability to do their job,

CASE STUDY

TAILORED TRAINING

In late 1996, following the appointment of a new chief executive, the Central Office for Information (COI) implemented a programme to improve and update all IT. Its aim was to bring everybody within the organisation to the same level of IT capability and competence.

Before any training took place, however, the training provider carried out a training needs analysis to determine the specific needs of the staff. "We needed a very comprehensive, yet flexible package," explains COI's IT training project manager Inés Evans.

COI used the same independent systems services provider to provide the IT and to project manage the training of its 320 personnel. This enabled it to ensure that staff would only be given new equipment once they had the necessary skills to use it. Working around COI's equipment update schedule, the training provider taught staff in several UK locations.

"The needs analysis process highlighted the diverse level of IT skills among staff, which ranged from very little familiarity with PCs to advanced use of Microsoft Office," says Evans.

As a result, the training provider devised a number of core courses, starting with a basic introduction to PCs covering different aspects of Microsoft Word and PowerPoint, followed by advanced training in macro design and Microsoft Excel 97.

and training should be available to those who want it. Of course, there should be some degree of regulation: your training provider should work with you to ensure that the training requested meets the needs of the business.

The personnel records on every employee should include a training needs analysis (TNA), an audit of the existing skills of every individual that is updated as courses are completed and at every appraisal. Part of the skill of constructing a TNA is knowing the objectives of the business, so that the training manager can ensure that staff collectively possess the skills necessary for the company to grow and prosper. A TNA also helps measure the effectiveness of training, showing whether or not an individual's skills improved after they attended a course.

OPEN OR BESPOKE COURSES?

Sometimes an individual can find what he or she is looking for from public courses. Many training providers run these several times a year, at convenient locations around the country. However, it may be that your employees need training in bespoke applications or specific business processes, or that they cannot make the dates of public courses.

Commissioning a specially-constructed programme or project may be your only option. Your training "tailor" should be big enough and experienced enough for you to have confidence in its ability to deliver the right training at the right time to the right people in the right way.

As mentioned earlier, it is crucial that it fully understands your business and the skills that are required by the individual and the organisation. A sophisticated trainer not only develops

WHAT TO LOOK FOR AND WHERE TO FIND IT

Have you checked whether your potential training providers are accredited? Your trainer should have been accredited by one or more of the following:

- Lotus Authorised Technical Education Centre (LAEC).

- Novell Authorised Education Centre (NAEC).

- Microsoft Certified Education Centre (CTEC). This replaces the ATEC label in 1999.

- Accredited Training Provider – Institute of IT Training.

- Seagate Authorised Training Centre.

One of the easiest methods of tracking down these accreditation bodies is via the Internet. Try the following Web sites:

- www.microsoft.com/train_cert/

- www.education/novell.com/certification

- www.lotus.com

- www.iitt.org.uk

tailored courses but also decides on the most effective way of delivering them. If, for example, directors find it difficult to balance their need to attend courses with their day-to-day commitments at the office, a compromise might be to set up a dedicated training room on-site.

SUPPORT MATERIALS

Whether they travel to a special location or receive training on-site, employees will need:

- *A dedicated PC, terminal or Macintosh;*

- *A comfortable workstation;*

- *Easy-to-use course material.*

All these can be provided by the right training organisation – along, of course, with a good teacher. Electronic media mean, however, that the physical presence of an instructor is becoming less essential. Computer based training (CBT) is another alternative for busy executives, allowing them to access course material when and where they want to and to go back over sections as many times as they want. Completed modules can be uploaded electronically and checked and marked by a tutor. Alternatively, the process can be entirely self-monitored.

As you would expect, IT is itself an important tool for the IT trainer. The Internet and intranets are increasingly being used to deliver interactive training programmes as well as the course literature that would otherwise have to be printed centrally and distributed to training locations. In other words, there are now many alternatives to the traditional "chalk and board" methods, and these can be adapted to meet the needs of your employees and organisation. You may even feel you need a provider that can offer one-to-one training – either for those personnel too busy and too important to break their commitments and join a group or for employees who have very specific needs, not shared by anyone else in the company. Be warned, however: not every provider is able to deliver one-to-one training at a cost-effective price.

KEEPING TRAINING ON TRACK

The actual training process is only part of the training story. Behind the scenes, enormous effort is required to ensure that the content of courses meets requirements, that the trainers are good, and that the candidates get to the end of a course with skills and benefits that they will retain. It looks easy but it isn't – it's a complex and time-consuming element of any training project.

The training administrator is responsible for creating a schedule of course dates, distributing course descriptions and pre-course questionnaires, taking bookings and sending out joining instructions, maintaining course attendance records, recording course feedback and providing the information for training review meetings.

CONSULTANTS: THE KEY INFLUENCES

The individual consultant actually creating and delivering the course to your employees is obviously the most important element of the training package, and it is critical that their knowledge, presentation skills and approach match the course attendees' requirements.

Having the right training consultant can make the difference between good and bad training: if the trainer designs a course that is relevant and enjoyable staff will be more likely to remember what they learn. Check that a provider demands the highest standards of its key personnel.

Training consultants should:

■ *Have attended comprehensive "train-the-trainer" courses;*

■ *Be able to present technical knowledge clearly;*

■ *Be expected to attend courses with the leading software houses to ensure their skills remain current and of the highest quality;*

■ *Be able to present formal certification in their specialist areas;*

■ *Be regularly monitored to ensure they continue to deliver the best to delegates.*

NINE ATTRIBUTES OF A GOOD PROGRAMME

When making decisions about staff training you should bear in mind:

- **Quality control**
  Your provider should be able to monitor and measure the effectiveness of its courses. It should also ensure that your company's decision makers understand the technology issues of the day and that end-users know how the features and short-cuts of the relevant software packages work.

- **Certification**
  It is essential that your support staff receive the best technical training available. Courses developed by software vendors offer formal certification, proving that delegates have reached an industry-recognised level of skills. These should be available to your technical staff.

- **Cost-effectiveness**
  Schemes such as volume discounts and training vouchers will help ensure that you get real value for money. Remember, however, that an effective training programme will reduce the overall cost of ownership of your IT by making users less dependent on formal and informal support structures.

- **Range of courses**
  Your provider's portfolio should include systems courses on Microsoft Windows NT and Novell NetWare and application courses on Lotus Notes and SmartSuite and Microsoft Office. It should encompass all the strategic IT platforms and all the leading software applications.

- **Tailoring**
  Choose a trainer that can deliver specially tailored and modified courses to meet the needs of your employees and organisation.

- **Accessibility**
  If employees are unable to attend the regular public courses, you will need a provider that can deliver courses either at easily accessible dedicated premises or your own site.

- **Expertise**
  Ensure that the trainers are themselves properly trained. Software vendors' accreditations and process control approvals such as ISO9001 are a good guide to the provider's standard.

- **Imagination**
  Training should be interactive and fun if it is going to be effective. You need to look for a training provider that works hard at creating an atmosphere conducive to learning.

- **Reputation**
  There is nothing like a series of happy customers to give you confidence. Your provider should be willing to put you in touch with past and current clients who can vouch for its expertise and flexibility.

PREPARATION AND FEEDBACK

Ideally, your provider should run a pilot course to test the validity of content and training methods. The pilot should then be evaluated, and there should be scope for fairly dramatic modifications if necessary.

After training has been completed there should be a procedure for follow-up to determine whether individuals are satisfied with the courses they have attended and believe the skills they have acquired are relevant to their job and their career path. This kind of follow-up not only means courses can be fine-tuned for future trainees but also helps highlight any gaps that still exist in the knowledge of a course "graduate". A good training provider will deliver this kind of post-training consultancy as part of its package.

Chapter 9

The case for out-tasking

Maximum control of strategy but minimum involvement in day-to-day troubleshooting is the goal of the modern IT manager. Nick Langley, technology writer looks at why using a number of specialist contractors can help achieve it

In IT services there is a move away from "one-stop shopping" to a "best of breed" approach. While dealing with a single outsourcing supplier has some benefits, mostly to do with simplicity of administration, organisations are increasingly recognising that using a number of specialist providers for their desktop, data centre and telecommunications requirements leads to greater efficiencies and better service.

According to market analysts International Data Corporation (IDC), 80 per cent of companies believe that outsourcing individual functions offers more benefits than paying a single outsourcing company to take over the work of the whole IT department.

The trend has much to do with increasing recognition of IT as central to the performance and objectives of the business. During the late eighties and early nineties, organisations were happy to hand over what they saw as a peripheral function or a problematic overhead to a specialist: if a single outside company took care of IT for them they could get on with their core business. In addition, the economies of scale offered by a large outsourcing supplier could mean that the cost of a contract was less than providing the service in-house.

Nowadays, IT is seen as an integral part of the core business at every level – be it shop-floor production or the customer services department. As such, it must be directly and fully controlled by management.

In the past, many outsourcing contracts were formed for the wrong reasons: to get rid of a "problem", or to save money, rather than to achieve business benefits and improvements in quality of service for users. As one market analyst puts it: "Sole sourcing can seldom be justified unless the client heavily invests in active management and controls throughout the contract's term. This never happens in real life."

A survey by the research group OTR provides an interesting parallel for IDC's findings, confirming that single sourcing is becoming anachronistic. OTR says the supplier marketplace has fragmented into specialists, with no single supplier providing a comprehensive range of "best of breed" services. OTR concludes that companies that want to keep their business processes in-house, but outsource specific IT functions, can obtain better value from a number of specialist providers.

In June 1998, *Computer Weekly* quoted Alisdair Henderson-Begg, director of the outsourcing consultancy TBI, and previously head of IT at British Aerospace, as saying: "The single, monolithic outsourcing contract is a myth. Even a giant supplier which is a single contractor will use a lot of sub-contractors".

The decision facing the client organisation, according to Henderson-Begg, is whether to let a prime contractor look after IT and deal with the other sub-contractors, or to deal directly with various suppliers themselves.

THE NEED FOR EXTERNAL HELP

"Never has the network manager lived in such interesting times," declares the network auditing specialist Pinpoint Software in the introduction to a survey of the network management practices of 1,000 corporate and public-sector organisations. "On the one hand, the user community is screaming that the network is mission-critical and if it fails to provide adequate (but often ill-defined) service levels, the network manager's job is on the line.

"On the other hand, his or her job is also on the line if costs aren't kept strictly under control...It would help if the existing infrastructure was beyond reproach, but most network managers have inherited a heterogeneous collection of PCs, most of which aren't powerful enough to run the latest software and many of which don't appear on any asset list (at least, not in the location documented). Even the scope of the problem is somewhat ill-defined, because important systems run on PCs that aren't attached to the network."

Pinpoint found that approximately 90 per cent of the network manager's time was spent on day-to-day tasks and "firefighting", leaving just ten per cent for strategy and forward planning. This is where out-tasking can help, by freeing managers to concentrate on developing IT strategies that better support the business.

DISTINGUISHING OUT-TASKING FROM OUTSOURCING

The goals of outsourcing and out-tasking are the same. Both provide agreed levels of service at fixed or agreed costs. But in the case of outsourcing, the service company actually takes ownership of assets such as servers, desktop systems and networks. The outsource service provider may also take ownership of software and be allowed to maintain or replace it as it chooses, provided the service levels are met. It may even take over the client's IT staff.

In out-tasking, the processes are carried out by the service provider, but the client continues to own the assets. The out-tasking service provider works for the client's IT function, leaving the client's IT management to concentrate on business objectives. Among other benefits are that:

- *Supplementing core IT staff, the client gets access to a specialist workforce of hundreds or thousands – although they will be supported by a dedicated project team;*

- *The client can be sure of best practice, laid down by years of experience of dozens of contracts;*

- *Being service organisations, out-tasking companies are flexible, used to responding quickly to changing customer needs and new business models;*

■ *Because they work for many large clients, out-tasking companies are likely to have closer relations with manufacturers such as Microsoft and better access to their expertise than the client organisation.*

The service supplier will have its own processes – perhaps even its own software – for managing and delivering IT services both on-site and remotely. It in turn may have a relationship with a specialist, which can provide the systems and network management tools to address procurement, installation, moves and changes and asset management, as well as remote systems monitoring.

CASE STUDY

CASTING THE NET WIDE

Two years ago, Cellnet signed a managed services contract with a leading independent systems services provider.

The ever-increasing rate of change in the cellular technology industry means that companies such as Cellnet have enough to do to meet customers' expectations.

"Five years ago our business was 99 per cent about delivering communications technology," explains Wendy Harmsworth, Cellnet's head of service management. "Today it is much more IT related with the pursuit of voice, data, fax and Internet connectivity."

"We realised that there were opportunities to improve service delivery – not on numbers, but on service levels," says Harmsworth. Working closely together with its out-tasking provider, Cellnet secured a contract that covered a broad span of functions:

■ Hardware maintenance for PCs, laptops and servers; and

■ Personal support services through a dedicated team of second and third-line staff.

"We wanted to get rid of the pain, so we looked for an arrangement where we could decide our requirements and it would be somebody else's job to deliver them," says Harmsworth. "I have no regrets. Our business is delivering communications; theirs is supplying and supporting desktop PCs. We now have a ready supply of up-to-date IT experts who hit the ground running."

Economies of scale will be passed down to the client: by servicing a large number of customers, the supplier shares the cost of the solutions over a number of its customers, thereby adding value to each relationship.

Measuring the costs and value of desktop assets is one of the main areas where an out-tasking company can help its clients. Generally, cost savings are made during the later stages of an out-tasking contract, when the client can save between 10 and 25 per cent compared with the cost of providing services internally.

THE VALUE OF DESK-TOP ASSETS

The first job of the out-tasking service provider, before service levels can be discussed, will be to establish a true picture of the IT assets of the client organisation.

Compared with mainframes and other data-centre based computing resources, desktop assets, which may have been acquired piecemeal over the years, are hard to keep track of. Some departments may have gone their own way. Even where a company has a centrally managed policy for its desktop technology, different generations of hardware and different versions of operating systems and application software may be in use.

In its recent survey of 1,000 corporate and public sector organisations, Pinpoint Software found that 89 per cent of network managers were unable to give an accurate figure for the number of PCs currently installed on their network. Fifty five per cent could only give an estimate to the nearest ten. Four per cent could only do so to the nearest 500.

Even when organisations have an up-to-date picture of their desktop assets, they may be measuring their value by the wrong yardsticks.

Many organisations calculate the depreciation of desktop technology in terms appropriate to mainframe computers, where a write-down period of three or five years may be realistic. Desktop technology changes so quickly that three years is probably too long, 18 months closer to the mark. For example, now that Microsoft has released its Windows 98 operating system, support for its predecessor, Windows 95, is certain to be withdrawn. Typically, support for older releases stops within a year of a new edition being declared stable.

DEMARCATION BETWEEN SERVICE PROVIDERS

Each client organisation will have a different mix of technology. Even if its preferred platform is NT, there may be pockets of Unix. The PC network may be linked to the private branch exchange (PBX) to support call-centre functions such as telesales or customer support.

The out-tasking service provider will manage some or all of these technologies: the cabling, the data switches, the servers, the gateways, hubs, routers, network printers and individual desktops. However, there will come a point at which another out-tasking specialist will need to take over, for example, in the management of the mainframe or telecoms network. It is very rare for the organisation that manages the mainframe to subcontract out the desktop to another service provider.

Responsibilities may be assigned by a joint management services forum, including representatives of the client, the telecoms company and the out-tasking companies looking after the desktop and the data centre.

The forum establishes procedures for managing the interface between the different service providers, often using models established in other projects. By analysing the processes and looking at the responsibility and escalation paths the group is able to ensure that the rules of ownership are clearly defined. After all, disputes between providers that force the client to intervene are in no-one's interests.

THE OUT-TASKING PROCESS

The out-tasking process typically begins with a due diligence and negotiation phase, during which the service provider acquires the necessary understanding of the client's business goals and service levels are agreed.

This is followed by an implementation phase, when

responsibility is handed over from the client or another third party to the service provider. At the end of this phase, which typically takes around three months, the service comes under the new provider's control.

Over the next six months the service provider will work on bringing the hardware and software up to a common standard, stablising the networking infrastructure and installing the software "agents" that make remote management possible.

Occasionally some users or groups of users who have gone their own way will be reluctant to move to the standards the provider wishes to implement. This is usually resolved by the company themselves. However, if this proves problematic, the the service provider should be prepared to discuss the issue directly with the company's business managers and agree a timeframe to get them moved from one platform to another.

ONSITE OR OUT OF SIGHT

Out-tasking services are divided between those delivered at the client's site and those provided remotely from the out-tasking company's support centre. Installations, decommissioning, site surveys for procurement, moves and changes and hardware repairs clearly require an on-site team.

Help desk and problem resolution services can be delivered by the phone or e-mail, and diagnostic tools can be used to detect and resolve hardware and software faults remotely over the network.

The network will be continuously monitored using intelligent agents, which can detect faults or network or storage capacity overloads so that they can be put right before they become a problem for users. In some cases, the technology will be able to detect and resolve problems and restart processes without manual intervention.

The support centre will also collect statistics that can be used in capacity planning or to detect and resolve underlying problems or persistent faults – be they in the networking infrastructure or an individual PC.

KEY POINTS

■ Service quality can be improved by selecting specialist companies to support different aspects of an organisation's IT requirements, rather than outsourcing all IT functions to one supplier.

■ Out-tasking companies work for the customer's IT organisation, instead of taking over its function as outsourcing companies do. This frees IT management to concentrate on strategic and business issues.

■ A management forum including representatives of the customer and the different out-tasking companies co-ordinates the activities of all parties.

■ Few organisations have an accurate picture of their desktop assets and so most find it difficult to impose standards and manage services consistently. Out-tasking companies have the skills and tools to do this.

■ Once standards and management systems are in place, the quality both of day-to-day service and long-term planning is improved.

■ While the biggest benefits are in service quality improvement, an out-tasking customer can ultimately save 10-25 per cent of the cost of providing services internally.

Glossary of terms

Channel assembly	A programme that enables an organisation that purchases IT equipment from manufacturers or distributors to perform final assembly of key components of a PC.
Desktop	Computer technology that is configured for direct use by employees.
Distributed IT or computing	Computer systems in multiple locations throughout an organisation working in a co-operative fashion. The system at each location serves the needs of that location, but is also able to receive information from other systems and to supply information to other systems within the network.
Electronic commerce	Commercial transactions performed electronically, ie. over the Internet or modem lines
Network computer	A network computer is similar to a PC which runs a small operating system in memory, but has no local storage space.
Out-task	The sub-contracting of discrete activities by organisations to external service providers.
Outsource	The sub-contracting of management operations by organisations to external service providers to perform entire functions, thereby replacing in-house functions.
Reseller	An organisation that purchases IT equipment from manufacturers or distributors and resells products to end-user organisations.
Server	A system or programme that receives requests from one or more client systems or programmes to perform activities that allow the client to accomplish certain tasks.
Time to desk	The lapse of time between a particular need for a PC being identified and that need being fulfilled with a working system on the desk of the user.
Vendor independent	A term used to describe a marketing stance which is not aligned with any particular manufacturer.